Introduction t

For Non-English

Speakers

By

Angelina Johnson

In conjunction with

Andrea Conrad

First Published   2008

Published by A and A works
Angelina   Johnson and Andrea Conrad
Altrincham,   England.
Info@AandAworks.co.uk

A note from the authors

Travelling away from home to work, for the first time can be a big step and a little worrying. The first time we travelled away from home we were not sure if we had made the right decision, only time would tell.

We created this book for all those people who need a 'kick start' with developing their English language skills when working with children. Personalize the book, keep it with you at all times, use it as a reference and see how quickly you learn. You will find lots of practical advice alongside a wealth of extremely useful vocabulary.

Caring for children in another country has given both myself and Andrea some of the most memorable times of our lives while learning a new language quickly has given us valuable skills which we have used in many areas of our lives.

Have a great time and most of all have fun!!!

Angelina and Andrea

This book belongs to

Name

....

....

Emergency services 999
(Police, fire and Ambulance service)

Contact details

Home

....

Mobile

....

Work

....

Contents Page

Routines

- **Daily**
- **Morning**
- **Afternoon**
- **Bath time**
- **Bed time**

Daily routine

A routine is the order in which things happen.

A healthy routine must include fresh air, exercise, a balanced diet, sleep and rest and the opportunity to play, on their own, with adults and other children.

Routines help babies and children understand the world around them.

Morning routine

When the children get up in the morning they may have breakfast,

 have a wash,

brush their teeth then

get dressed.

Children need a daily routine so they know what is happening and when. A routine helps babies and children feel safe and secure in their environment.

Afternoon routine

When children arrive home from school/Nursery they will be hungry, a healthy snack will help get them through to supper (Evening meal)

Older children will need to do their homework before playing otherwise they will become too tired later in the evening.

Younger children may need to have an afternoon nap (sleep).

When babies' and young children become tired they will become easily upset.

It is important to make sure the child does not sleep to late in the afternoon otherwise they will not want to go to bed in the evening.
Having a set time for afternoon sleeps/naps will help maintain the child's routine, helping to avoid tears and tantrums from over tired toddlers.

 It is important to recognize the signs of tiredness in babies and young children.
Children who are tired may become upset easily, be difficult to settle, crying a lot, rubbing their eyes, suck their thumb and pulling at their ears.

It is important that children have regular fresh air and exercise as part of their daily routine. Fresh air helps the child concentrate and aids good sleep Patterns.

By following certain rules like washing hands before meals, will help children to learn from what they see around them. Following routines will also help children develop independence, this means doing things by themselves, children enjoy being independent and able to do things for themselves, it is also an important skill to learn before going to school.

Babies and children need their routine to be individual to them.

Bed time routine

It is very important to make sure children are not excited before they go to bed, if children are allowed to play active games before going to bed they will find it difficult to settle down.

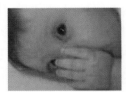

Children will need down time from any activities before they go to bed, this will help with settling then to sleep.

A bath  and a story

with a grownup are a good way to calm children after a busy day before going to bed.

It is important to make sure children brush their teeth before going to bed. It is a good idea to introduce babies to the tooth brush as soon as they start to get their first teeth. This will help teeth brushing to become a part of daily life.

Hygiene

- **Personal Hygiene**
- **Children's Hygiene**

Children hygiene

Baby

It is very important to keep babies and children clean to protect them from illness caused by **germs and bacteria**.

It is ok for children to get messy from time to time but cleaning them up is very important .

Babies who do not move around much will need less bathing. They will need to be washed carefully daily in the morning and before they go to bed, at night

Not only will this keep baby clean but will help establish a routine, which is very important to babies and children.

Toddler (1--3 years)

Once babies start to move around they can get dirty, this means they will need to be **bathed more often.**

Babies (once moving) and toddlers will need to go in a bath daily and washed regularly throughout the day, to prevent them getting poorly from germs and bacteria.

You should also use a baby wash to clean the baby/child's skin and keep them smelling fresh.

When washing children you should use a

soft cloth/ flannel   to gently rub away any dirt / mess on the child's skin.

Older children

As with younger children they will on occasion get very dirty, especially after playing outside. It is especially important to make sure they are bathed at these times.

However older, more independent children may need bathing less often, they should however **bathe**

 or **wash**

carefully **daily.**

Older children may prefer to shower,

this is fine for older children.

It is not a good idea to shower younger children as the temperature can change suddenly which will **upset** young children at the least and **burn** their delicate skin at worse.

It is also important to make sure children

brush their teeth to keep their teeth and gums healthy and breath fresh.

Hair Care

Older children will need help in taking care of their **hair**. It is a good idea to use a gentle shampoo and conditioner as some shampoos contain chemicals which will sting the child's eyes.

Many young children become very upset when having their hair washed, as they do not like the water going in their eyes. A good way to deal with this is to use **SWIMMING GOGGLES** to protect the child's eyes, children will love this idea and hair washing will become

much more fun!

You must help children to brush their hair to keep it looking neat and tidy.

Little girls with long hair should have their hair tired in a pony tail when going to school or nursery, as this helps reduce the risk of **head lice**.

Head lice are sometimes called **Nits.** They live in the hair and are tiny bug like parasites.

There are **signs** to look for so you will know when children may have head lice.

Children will scratch their heads constantly as lice are very irritating.

It is important to check the child's hair regularly, as this can help in reducing the severity of it the outbreak of the head lice.

There are many over the counter

treatments which can be bought from the local Chemist / Pharmacy. This is an example of one such product

You will need to follow the directions carefully to make sure it works.
After using the lotion you will need to use a fine tooth comb like the one below to get out any remaining lice/eggs otherwise the problem will keep recurring.
Experts say it takes three (3), weeks to fully eradicate head lice with daily combining after treatment.

It is important to keep babies and children clean at all times to prevent illness from germs and Bacteria

Blouse

Cardigan

Dungarees

Dresses

Fleecy top

Flip Flops

Jeans

Jogging pants

Jumper

Knickers/ girls Underwear

Leggings

Pumps

Pinafore

Shorts

Skirt

Slipper

Socks

Girls

Boys

Sweatshirt

Tights

T-shirt

Tracksuit

Top **Bottoms**

Trousers

Girls

Boys

Underpants/boys
Boxer shorts

Vest

Vest top

Swimwear
Girl's swimming costume

Bikini

Swimwear
Boys
Trunks

Shorts

Swimming accessories

Safety jacket

Arm bands

Swim ring

Nightwear

Night dress

Pajamas

Sleep suit

For babies
Dressing gown/bath robe

Baby clothes
Baby grow

Body suit

Bootees

Bonnet

Cardigan

Day suit/rompers

Dresses

Hat

Scratch mittens

Shawl

OUTDOOR CLOTHES

Coat

Gloves

Mittens

Hats (summer)

  **Cap**

Winter

Jacket

Rain coat

Sandals

Girls

Boys
Shoes

Girls

boys

Snow suit

Trainers/
Running shoes

Wellington boots

Food and Nutrition

- **Sterilizing Equipment**
- **Weaning**
- **Healthy diets for toddlers and older children**

Food and nutrition

Babies and children need to eat a healthy balanced diet so they grow and develop into healthy young people.

Babies

For the first 3 /4 months babies will be

fed breast milk

or formula milk
which contain all the goodness and nutrients a young baby need.
All equipment used to feed babies formula milk **must** be sterilized to prevent baby getting poorly from germs and bacteria.

You will also need to use a solution like the ones below

You must sterilize all equipment which goes into the baby's mouth including soothers/dummies, spoons and bottles

Weaning

Between 12 and 16 weeks baby will need to be slowly and carefully introduced to solid food. This will still be liquid like and in very small amounts to start with.

Baby rice and rusk are the best thing to introduce to start with, as they are made up of milk, either breast or formula.

 Baby rice Rusk

You will need to add milk to both these mixes before giving to baby.

Then you can gradually introduce fruit and vegetables **one(1)at a time**. This is important to make sure the baby does not have any allergies to certain foods.

Once baby has had experience of more than one, 1, food you can start to mix food for example carrot and potatoes.

You must make sure baby has had all foods on their own before you start to mix foods together.

 **Fruit Vegetables**

All food must be pureed in a **blender**, like the one below before being offered to baby, in the early stages of weaning to **prevent choking**

Once baby has tried a particular food, carrots or Potatoes you can start to mix

them together.
Baby will need a very small amount to start with about the size of an ice cube this can be increased as and when baby is hungrier. You will know when the baby is hungry as they will look for more food when their food is finished, they may also become upset when you stop feeding. Between 6--9mths babies will want to hold the spoon themselves and try to pick up their food themselves. At this time it's a good idea to give baby "finger food". As they are better able to chew food.

Foods to avoid

Babies under 1 year should not be given eggs there is a risk of salmonella.

Peanut butter increases the risk of allergies in children under 1year.

By now baby needs to be sitting up when being fed, in a chair similar to the ones below

For baby who is not sitting up unsupported (alone)

For baby when sitting up unsupported (alone)
It is important to encourage baby to feed themselves so they can develop their co-ordination to improve and perfect this skill.

To make sure children grow and develop it is important to make sure they have a balanced diet.
A balanced diet must include

Carbohydrates

Bread   Pasta   Sugary foods

Protein

Fish   Chicken

Vitamins and minerals

Fruit   Vegetables

Diary

Milk, Cheese and Yogurt

Fats

Butter   Burgers

Each meal should contain something from each of the 5 food groups to help children grow and develop healthily.

We must limit the amount of fats and sugary foods babies and children have but we must **never** stop children having these foods altogether because they need them for energy and to grow

This is called a balanced diet.

Babies and children will sometimes not like or want the food they are offered at mealtimes, it is very important not to force children to eat this can cause lots of problems later.

If children choose not to eat their meal and are hungry later they should be offered a healthy snack **AVOID** giving treats to children if they don't eat at meal

times. A sandwich toast

or fruit will stop the child from being hungry.

You must always offer babies and

children a drink with their meal. The best

drink to offer is water although
some children will prefer Juice.

Try to avoid cordials, diluted
juices like orange / blackcurrant

as they have many additives
and are not good for the baby or child's
teeth

Never give juice to a baby/child in a

bottle a Sippy cup, with a lid is
best for young babies/ toddlers

This cup will help young babies
become independent in taking a drink
with out to much mess.

A Beaker cup is good for young children, who are better able to hold a cup without spilling.

Do not punish children for not eating a meal. If you make a fuss children will quickly realize they can gain attention from meal times / food, which is not healthy in any way!

Keeping children safe in the home

- The lounge
- The Kitchen
- The bedroom
- The bathroom

Safety in the lounge

When caring for young children it is important to ensure that the environment is safe, so babies and children don't hurt themselves on everyday objects around the home.

A good example of this is do not leave hot drinks on a low coffee table.

Adding **corner covers** to sharp edges on low tables will help prevent mobile toddlers from hurting themselves when they fall over.

Another potential danger to babies and small children in the sitting room/playroom are **plug sockets**. Small fingers can easily poke the holes in plug sockets.
The best way to prevent (stop) this is to cover all plug sockets when not in use. It is very important to make sure you replace plug socket covers if removed for any reason.

Plug socket cover

Clutter on the floor can make it difficult for babies and children to move around .It can also be the cause of accidents. It is important to tidy toys away when children have finished Playing, to prevent children tripping and hurting themselves.

It is a good idea to encourage children to help tidy up their toys as this will help them take ownership of their belongings.

Keeping the environment tidy will help keep it clean and free from germs and bacteria.
You should use a gentle cleaner which will not cause harm to babies and small children.

The areas in the home where children play must be clean and tidied daily.
The items below will be useful in keeping the home clean and tidy.

Hoover   Mop   bucket

Chair

Coffee table

Computer

D.V.D

Keyboard

Radiator

Rug

Sofa

Television

Accidents at home

It is important to identify dangers in the home before they cause harm to children. The best way to do this is to recognize hazards / dangers at home. By recognizing what is dangerous we can keep the home safe therefore ensuring children stay safe.

It is important to know what to do in an emergency and when you need to ask for help. If in doubt check it out, don't leave things to chance.

Safety in the Kitchen

The kitchen is a dangerous place for young children, therefore it is important to follow a few simple rules.

When cooking you must **not** allow children into the kitchen, a safety gate at the kitchen door is a useful way to keep children out , safe yet still be able to see

you.  Always turn pan

handles
towards the back of the cooker,

Hob (top of cooker) when
cooking. Household rubbish can cause
germs and bacteria. It is important to
empty the kitchen bin regularly.

Having high standards of personal
hygiene will also help to keep the babies
and children in your care safe and
healthy.

Bowl

Chair

Colander

Cooker

Cupboard

Cup

Dining Table

Dish washers

Fish slice

Freezer

Frying pan

Fridge

Fork

Jug

Knife

Glasses

Measuring spoons

Microwave

Plates

Plug

Plug socket

Potato masher

Rubbish bin

Rolling pin

Sauce pan

Spoon

Soup ladle

Sink

Tap

Tumble dryer

Washing machine

Whisk

Wooden spoon

Safety in the bedroom

Bedrooms can also be hazardous places for small children.

It is very important to make sure the bedroom is set up in a way which will not create dangers for young children.

Young children like to climb and jump, therefore they must never be left to play alone for long periods of time in the bedroom.

Furniture must not be placed close to windows. Windows must have a safety lock on them to stop children opening it and falling out.

 **Window lock**

Young children may also need a bed guard to stop them from falling out

Bed guard

It is very important to make sure the floor space is clear from clutter, toys, clothes, shoes, especially at night time, in case children wake and get out of bed.
Clear floor space is very important to prevent accidents from tripping, should anyone need to get out of bed in the night, or need to evacuate in the case of an emergency, like in a fire.

Bed

Bedside lamp

Bedside table

Coat/clothes hangers

Dressing table

Duvet

Duvet cover

Mirror

Pillow

Pillow case

Sheet

Wardrobe

Bathroom safety

Young children love water, which makes the bathroom a dangerous place for unsupervised children.

Babies and children must **NEVER** be left alone in the bath or shower.

You must make sure children do not play with items stored in the bathroom like razors, shampoo, bubble bath or cleaning materials.

Many of the everyday products we store in the bathroom can cause serious harm to young children therefore it is very important to store them safely on a high shelf or locked cupboard.

Bath tub

Bath toys

Boat

Bubble bath

Conditioner

Duck

Face cloth/
Flannel

Nail brush

Laundry Basket

Shampoo

Scissors

Shower

Shower gel

Toilet

Toilet roll (tissue)

Toilet roll holder

Towel

Towel rail

Soap

Soap/Soap dispenser

Keeping children safe outside the home

- **Gardens**
- **Busy roads**
- **Parks**
- **Planning a trip**

Gardens

Gardens can be hazardous places for unsupervised children. It is important to follow a few simple rules to keep children safe from accidents in the garden.

Gates must be kept closed at all times to stop children from getting onto busy roads.

Fences must be secure to stop children getting out of the garden and stray animals getting in.

Garden tools must be stored in a safe place, like a garden shed, with a lock on it.

Plants and flowers should be planted and chosen carefully to make sure there are no poisonous/dangerous plants or flowers in the garden where children play. Children should not be allowed to put anything from the garden into their mouth.

Busy roads

All roads a are dangerous to young children, not least because children do not recognise dangers. You must always cross the road at a **crossing**.

You must always hold the child's hand while crossing the road. You must **NEVER** allow children to cross the road between parked car.

Teach children the following rules of crossing the road.

Parks

It is important to Keep children safe when in outdoor spaces, especially in public parks.
Children are particularly vulnerable to Strangers. A stranger is anyone you don't know.

Discarded litter, broken play equipment and stray animals are all hazardous to babies and children in public parks.
It is very important to make sure you are Are very careful with small children and strangers animals, the animal may not be used to small children touching it, the little fingers of young children could frighten the animal causing it to scratch

or bit the child.

Planning a trip

Here are some general guidelines to help you when planning a trip out either with the baby/ child in you care, with friends or alone.

- ✓ Always tell someone where you are going and when to expect you back.
- ✓ Keep your mobile phone on at all times
- ✓ Think about where you are going, how you are getting there and back.
- ✓ Enquire about transport in advance, if it is needed.

When taking babies or children out for a longer than usual time you must consider the following:

Meal time, will you need to take food,

snacks or drinks with you?

Nap/sleep times is the child likely to
need a sleep while you are out.

Nappy changes, for babies, always
take more than you think you will
need in case you get held up and are out
longer than you expect

Is your trip likely to require a change of
clothes? Fresh underwear for toddlers

A coat   or a sun hat
Depending on the weather

When you are taking a baby or child out of the house you **MUST** always tell someone where you are going. Parents can quickly become anxious if they don't know where you and their children are.

If the child is not a good walker or has not been walking for long it is important to take a push chair with you otherwise the child could very quickly become tired and distressed, which can be very stressful to you the carer   and a tired and grumpy child.

Behaviour management

- ### Reward ideas

Behaviour management

It is very important to encourage children to behave appropriately, in a way we would like them to.
The best way to do this is to praise children when they behave well.
This helps children feel good about themselves.

Children learn how to behave from what they see, therefore it is very important to show children how to behave at all times.
If you yell (shout) at them they will often yell back.

This is not a good example to children!

It is very important to remain calm when dealing with small children.

A good way to help children understand the rules of being good is to use rewards and positive praise.

The rewards don't need to be big to encourage children to behave appropriately. A simple star chart and praise will often work.

Star charts are a very good way of encouraging young children to behave appropriately, with a small treat when an agreed number of stars have been achieved, children will soon enjoy behaving appropriately and following rules.

Play, toys and activities

- **0—6Mths**
- **6—12Mths**
- **1—3Yrs**
- **3—5Yrs**

Play 0--6months

Very young babies need to be entertained, talked to and played with. This will help them develop an understanding of the world around them. Young babies will need a range of toys which stimulate their sense

Toys/items which will stimulate the following senses?

Vision **Smell**

Touch **Hearing**

It is important to clean all toys regularly

This helps to kill any germs on the toys

Useful activities for a baby between birth and 6months

Going out for a walk to the park

Musical toys and rattles

Mobiles

Soft toys (Teddy bear)

6--12months

Babies of this age are now starting to become mobile, moving around

They will therefore need to be entertained and watched carefully all the time.

Children of this age enjoy exploring their environment therefore general household items will often be as much fun as any expensive toys
These items can be a lot of fun and are safe for a baby to play with.

You must never leave a baby or small child alone!

It is important to encourage babies to move around as much as possible.

A good way to do this is place objects they like just beyond their reach, brightly coloured toys and household objects will encourage them to start to move, however you **must not** allow the baby to become upset.

1--3 year olds

Children of this age are wanting to be a little more independent, therefore will benefit from activities and toys which will allow this.

However children must not be left to play alone for long periods of time as interaction is very important for the development of social and language skills

The following **indoor activities** will give a good balance of independent and adult lead play

Imaginative play

Puzzles

Board games

Painting

Picture dominos game
Snap cards

Play dough

Lego/duplo

Play 3--5 years

Children within this age range are developing the skills they have already acquired.

For their skills to continue to develop children will need to spend time with other children of their own age **AND** adults. Children learn from what they see, so must always be set a good example.

It is also important for children to learn how to share, a skill which can take some time to master. For this reason children will need to spend time with other children on a regular basis. Local playgroups are an excellent way to do this, taking children to playgroup will also give you the opportunity to meet other people and make new friends.

Children will continue to play with the toys and games we have already looked at but will benefit from continued adult Involvement.

Drawing, painting and colouring will also help develop the skills children need to learn how to write, therefore should be encouraged.

Board games will help children with the important skill of sharing and taking turns. These activities are a great way to develop language and early reading skills.

It is important to make sure games are appropriate for the age of the child, if toys and games are too difficult children will quickly lose interest and not want to play.

All toys and games have an age range on them.

Toys and games will also carry the British Standard safety mark to show they have been check by the authority to ensure the safety of children and those playing with them.

Look out for the following signs and symbols when choosing toys for children.

Shows toys and games are checked to British Safety Standards.

This sign tells you toys and games are not suitable for very young children, may have small parts or loose, small pieces.

This is what you might see on the box or packaging of toy or game which is following all the required safety checks in Britain.

Bike/Bicycle

Board games

Books

Colouring book

Crayons

Desk

Doll

Football

Puzzle

skipping rope

Teddy Bear

Toys

Tricycle

Pram

Common Childhood illnesses

Childhood illnesses

From time to time children become unwell.

Generally they can be treated with over the counter remedies like the ones below which will help to reduce fevers. (temperature)

 **Paracetamol**

It is important to make sure medicine given is appropriate for the age of the child you are giving it too.

However sometimes you will need to consult a doctor therefore it is important to know the signs and symptoms of different illnesses.

Teething

Although not an illness, it is very painful for babies.

When babies start to cut their teeth this

is called teething. This is very painful for babies and can often cause a temperature. During this time it can be a good idea to use some form of pain relief Calpol or Calpofen are very effective also the use of a soothing gel will help make a baby feel more comfortable, like the ones shown.

Some common childhood illnesses

Colic *often occurs in babies from 6 weeks to 3 Months old babies. Baby becomes very unsettled often in the evening, this is caused through trapped wind. The use of colic drops may help to relieve the trapped wind. Drops should be given before the milk for bottle fed babies, this way it starts to work immediately as wind starts to build up.*

Nursing children on their tummy can also help release the trapped wind.
Sitting baby upright after feeding and rubbing their back may also help reduce the build up of wind after every feed, therefore reducing the risk of COLIC.

Chicken pox

Starts with a rash around the head and behind the ears, then pink spots appear in clusters (together), which become blisters. When the spots scab over they are no longer infectious. Children will often have a temperature/fever and feel unwell. The best treatment is calamine lotion. Apply with cotton wool to soothe the itch from the spots last 2--3 weeks.

Ear infection

Children will complain of a pain in their ear and or neck, behind the ear. Very young babies will their ear and cry a lot they will also have a fever which will cause them to be quite unsettled. The fever can be treated with calpol and rest , if symptoms persist the child must see the doctor for antibiotics.

Sore throat

Children will have difficulty swallowing, will not want to eat, have a fever and appear unsettled. Offer lots of drinks and regular pain relief, approximately every 4 hours if they have a fever. If symptoms persist the child will need to visit the doctor to rule out an infection.

Common cold

Children will have a runny nose, a fever and generally feel unwell. The best treatment plenty of drinks and rest.
If symptoms continue or worsen you should consult a doctor.

Meningitis

Starts with similar symptoms as a common cold, temperature/fever, runny nose, tiredness/drowsiness feeling sick /vomiting, dislike of lights, stiff neck, pain in joints a rash which does not go if pressed. Symptoms need prompt action as this can be a very serious illness. Babies will arch their backs and have a shrill cry. Some children will not like the light. If a child has these symptoms they must see a doctor URGENTLY.

Measles

Generally unwell, fever, runny nose, red eyes and a cough. Blotchy rash starts behind the ears and face then spreads to the rest of the body and a dislike of bright lights. Treat with calpol for the fever and consult a doctor.

Whooping cough

Starts with a cold and a dry cough, the cough becomes more persistent with a whoop which is a deep inhalation of breath, the cough can last up to 1month. Consult a doctor immediately as antibiotics will be needed, lots of comfort will be needed as it can be frightening for young children. Sit children up when coughing offer lots of drinks and stay close to the child especially during the night.

Vomiting & Diarrhea

This is quite common in babies and children, as they are very susceptible to germs and bacteria which cause vomiting and diarrhoea.

Children should be given lots of drinks and light, dry food. If symptoms persist a diarolite drink will to prevent dehydration which occurs quickly in babies and children. If symptoms persist for more than 24 hours seek medical advice.

Asthma

Children who suffer from asthma will be treated under the direction of a doctor, it is very important that the directions are followed very carefully. It is important to make sure that the children play and sleep in a room which is as dust free as possible as dust can cause the condition to worsen. Older children will be treated with an inhaler.

Heat rash

Heat rash appears when a baby or child becomes very hot and sweaty. The best way to treat this condition is to keep the baby or child cool, bathe regularly in warm/cool water dress them in loose fitting clothes to avoid irritation.

Eczema

Is when the skin becomes dry and irritated. The skin will become red, dry and itchy. Children will scratch the skin, sometimes until it bleeds. It is important to ensure the skin is clean and moisturized regularly to prevent the condition worsening.

Body parts

Arm

Chest

Ears

Eyes

Fingers

Feet / Foot

Hand

Head

Knee

Leg

Mouth

Nose

Stomach / Tummy

Teeth

Throat

Toes

Tongue